HISTORY AND DESCRIPTION

TOY POODLE

While it is concluded by all authorities that the large-sized specimens of the breed are the older varieties, there is sufficient evidence to show that the Toy Poodle was developed only a short the first century, that are found along the shores of the Mediterranean, portray the Poodle very much as he is seen in the 20th century. Clipped to resemble the lion, he is not unlike some of the specimens seen at the earliest

ISABELLE FRANCAIS

The most refined of all purebred dogs, the Toy Poodle is an intelligent and colorful companion dog.

time after the breed assumed the general type in which it is known today. This type, incidentally, has changed less than that of almost any other breed. It is a dog that has come down to us as the ancients knew it. Refinements have been effected, but there has been no change in its essential characteristics.

Those bas-reliefs, dating from bench shows.

It is possible that in the dim past there was a link between the dog attributed to the Island of Melita—now known as the Maltese—and the Toy Poodle. Similarly, there probably was a relationship between the Poodle and the dog of Spain—the Spaniel. If not from the same progenitor, the paths of their ancestors must have crossed at some remote time.

The first concrete evidence of the existence of the Toy Poodle in England is not found until the 18th century, when a toy known as the "White Cuban" became exceedingly popular in England. It was a sleeve dog, which soon became the pet of every grand

The Continent had known the Toy Poodle several centuries before it came to England. There are line drawings by the great German artist Durer that definitely establish the breed in the 15th and 16th centuries. How long the dog had been known in Spain is problematical, but it was definitely the principal pet dog of

ISABELLE FRANCAIS

The Havanese of today, a toy breed from Cuba, may be the present-day version of the "White Cuban," a breed possibly responsible for the Poodle.

lady in the country. This breed's origin was attributed to the West Indian island of Cuba, when it travelled to Spain, and from there to England. Queen Anne had several of these dogs in her later years. She had first seen them about 1700 when there came to England a troop of performing dogs known as "The Ball of Little Dogs." These Toy Poodles were exceptionally well trained, and they danced to music in almost human fashion.

the latter 18th century. This is established through the paintings of the famous Spanish artist Goya. In many of his portraits of the ladies of the court may be seen excellent examples of the Toy Poodle as the pampered favorite during the reign of Louis XVI, about the same period.

Considerable mystery surrounds the "White Cuban." Subsequent histories of the dog leave no conviction that this breed was indigenous to Cuba. No doubt, specimens of the Poodle or the Maltese—possibly both—had been carried to the West Indies by early explorers and traders. According to Lloyd, the White Cuban was a cross between the German or French white-corded Poodles and the Maltese. These dogs were larger than the Maltese, and their cords trailed on the ground.

The Toy Poodle is credited with being the principal ancestor of the truffle dog of England. It is believed that the Toy Poodle was crossed with a small terrier to produce a dog that would be ideal for its strange occupation. The truffle is an edible fungus that is to this day considered a great delicacy.

The high prices it commanded

ISABELLE FRANCAIS

ISABELLE FRANCAIS

Modern-day truffle dogs from Italy are called Lagottos; in France they are called Truefflers. The similarities between the Lagotto and the Poodle are still obvious in general appearance, coat, keenness of nose and intelligence.

Many consider the Standard Poodle to be the real people-Poodle, though two are admittedly more a handful than most people can handle.

were so attractive that the hunting of truffles became a widespread trade, especially in certain parts of the Hampshire and Wiltshire. The difficulty of procuring truffles lay in the fact that the fungus grew underground. It had to be scented out by a dog so that the master could dig it out. The dogs had to be carefully trained, and usually they were white in color, because truffle hunting was done at night. The sagacity and the scenting powers of the Poodle were said to form a perfect compliment to the terrier's ability to go to earth.

The modern history of the Toy Poodle is a straight descent from the size of the Standard and

Miniature Poodles. Standards are 15 inches or more at the shoulder; Miniatures under 15 inches but over ten inches, while Toys are ten inches or under. The standard for all three is identical except for size. The so-called "White Cuban phase" of the breed is believed to have no influence on the present-day specimens. The dogs of the 18th century in England probably left few, if any, descendants.

The diminutive size of the Toy Poodle rather militates against his use in any sporting sense, but fanciers of the small dog credit him with carrying all the tendencies of the larger members of the breed. His intelligence also is regarded as similarly high.

MINIATURE AND STANDARD

The Poodle is one of the most intelligent of the canine race, having within its own breed great variations of character. In fact, there is something more human than canine about most Poodles, which makes them unique dogs and enchanting companions. The origin of the Poodle is a mystery, although it is supposed by many authorities to have originated in

ISABELLE FRANCAIS

The Miniature Poodle, standing between 10 and 15 inches, is the most popular of the three Poodle varieties—not too big or too small.

The Standard Poodle represents the breed in its most athletic and workman form, a real showman and companion, and usually an excellent parent.

Germany, where it is known as the *Pudel* or *Canis Familiaris Aquatius*. However, for many years it has been regarded as the national dog of France, where it was commonly used as a retriever as well as a traveling circus dog. In France it was, and is, known as the *Caniche*, which is derived from *chien canne* or duck dog. The English word poodle is the beginning of the 19th century; and, except that the Irish Water Spaniel is born with short hair on its face and tail, there is little difference between this ancient Irish dog and the Poodle.

Whatever its origin, the Poodle is a well-established breed, for— as far as standards and records show—it has scarcely changed through the centuries, and the

ROBERT PEARCY

Poodles were originally bred as duck dogs, as its French name *Caniche* indicates. Today's breed hunts duck very infrequently but still remains an active and hardy outdoor dog.

undoubtedly derived from the German *Pudel* and the expression "French" Poodle was undoubtedly adopted because of the breed's great popularity in France.

As a matter of fact, the unclipped Poodle of today bears a strong resemblance in type to the old rough-haired water dog of England as painted by Reinagle at various standards of different countries are much alike. The Poodles of today are a trifle higher on the leg, as well as longer and narrower in the head and muzzle than formerly. If this fashion in type does not become too exaggerated, it improves the natural grace and beauty of the breed.

The Irish Water Spaniel of today still possesses many similar traits with the Poodle: both breeds are excellent water dogs with curly water-proof coats and characteristic topknots.

THE BREED STANDARD

Official standards that give the requirements for the Poodle have been approved by all national kennel clubs. Despite differences in wording, those requirements are essentially the same. There are, however, some significant variances that must be noted, especially by the owner who is planning to show a Poodle on an international basis or become involved in serious breeding programs. For example, the American Kennel Club and The Kennel Club (of Great Britain) differ on the height limitations that separate the Poodle into the three varieties of Standard, Miniature, and Toy. Also, there is a strong British preference that Poodles be shown in the traditional lion clip, which is known in the United States as the "English Saddle" clip.

For the sake of brevity, only the American version appears in its complete form within this book; the British standard is then discussed in terms of major variations from the American requirements.

Breed standards are always

ISABELLE FRANCAIS

Elegant and perfect proportions clipped in the traditional fashion define the Poodle and give him his own distinction and dignity.

subject to change through review by the national breed club for each dog, so it is always wise to keep up with developments in a breed by checking the publications of your national kennel club.

AKC STANDARD FOR THE POODLE

General Appearance, Carriage and Condition— That of a very active, intelligent and elegant-appearing dog, squarely built, well proportioned, moving soundly and carrying himself proudly. Properly clipped in the traditional fashion and carefully groomed, the Poodle has about him an air of distinction and dignity peculiar to himself.

Size, Proportion, Substance— Size—The *Standard Poodle* is over 15 inches at the highest point of the shoulders. Any Poodle which is 15 inches or less at the shoulders shall be *disqualified* from competition as a Standard Poodle. The *Miniature Poodle* is 15 inches or under at the highest point of the shoulders, with a minimum height in excess of 10 inches. Any Poodle which is over 15 inches or is 10 inches or less at the highest point of the

ROBERT SMITH

Although the Poodle is recognized throughout the world, there are subtle differences in grooming and breeding from country to country. This Standard Poodle is competing at a dog show in Ireland.

shoulders shall be *disqualified* from competition as a Miniature Poodle. The *Toy Poodle* is 10 inches or under at the highest point of the shoulders. Any Poodle which is more than 10 inches at the highest point of the shoulders shall be *disqualified* from competition as a Toy Poodle. As long as the Toy Poodle is definitely a Toy Poodle, and the Miniature Poodle a Miniature Poodle, both in balance and proportion for the Variety, diminutive-ness shall be the deciding factor when all other points are equal. *Proportion*— To insure the desirable squarely built appearance, the length of the body measured from breastbone to the point of the rump approximates the height from the highest point of the shoulders to the ground. *Substance*—Bone and muscle of both forelegs and hind legs are in proportion to size of dog.

Head and Expression—
(a)*Eyes*—very dark, oval in shape and set far enough apart and positioned to create an alert intelligent expression. *Major Faults: Eyes round, protruding, large or very light.* **(b)** *Ears* hanging close to the head, set at or slightly below eye level. The ear leather is long, wide and thickly feathered, however, the ear fringe should not be of excessive length. **(c)** *Skull* moderately rounded, with a slight but definite stop. Cheekbones and muscles flat. Length from occiput to stop about the same length of muzzle. **(d)** *Muzzle* long, straight and fine, with slight chiseling under the eyes. Strong without lippiness. The chin definite enough to preclude snipiness. *Major fault: Undershot, overshot, wry mouth.*

Neck, Topline, Body—
Neck well proportioned, strong and long enough to permit the head to be carried high and with dignity. Skin snug at throat. The neck rises from strong, smoothly muscled shoulders. *Major fault: Ewe neck.* The **topline** is level, neither sloping nor roached, from the highest point of the shoulder to the base of the tail, with the

ROBERT SMITH

The muzzle is desirably long, straight and fine with slight chiseling under the eyes, which are very dark and oval in shape.

exception of a slight hollow just behind the shoulder. ***Body*** (a) Chest deep and moderately wide with well sprung ribs. (b) The loin is short, broad and muscular. (c) Tail straight, set on high and carried up, docked of sufficient length to insure a balanced outline. ***Major faults:*** *Set low, curled, or carried over the back.*

Forequarters—

Strong, smoothly muscled shoulders. The shoulder blade is well laid back and approximately the same length as the upper foreleg. ***Major fault:*** *Steep shoulder.* **(a)** ***Forelegs*** straight and parallel when viewed from the front. When viewed from the side the elbow is directly below the highest point of the shoulder. The pasterns are strong. Dewclaws may be removed.

Feet—

The feet are rather small, oval in shape with toes well arched and cushioned on thick firm pads. Nails short but not excessively

The forequarters are strong with smoothly muscled shoulders, the chest is deep and moderately wide, and the tail is straight and carried up.

JOHN R. QUINN

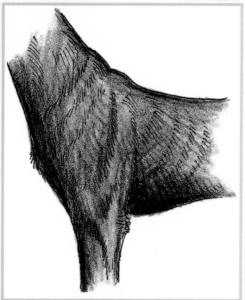

Steep shoulders are considered undesirable in the Poodle, as they can give the dog a somewhat short-necked appearance and shorten the length of the forequarters stride.

in tight even cords of varying length: longer on mane or body coat, head, and ears; shorter on puffs, bracelets, and pompons. **(b)***Clip*—A Poodle under 12 months may be shown in the "Puppy" clip. In all regular cases, Poodles 12 months or over must be shown in the "English Saddle" or "Continental" clip. In the Stud Dog and Brood Bitch classes and in a non-competitive Parade of Champions, Poodles may be shown in the "Sporting" clip. A Poodle shown in any other type of clip shall be *disqualified. (1)* ***"Puppy":*** A puppy under a year old may be shown in the "Puppy" clip with the coat long. The face, throat, feet and base of the tail are shaved. The entire shaven foot is visible. There is a pompon on the end of the tail. In order to give a neat appearance and a smooth, unbroken line, shaping of the coat

shortened. The feet turn neither in nor out. *Major faults: Paper or splay foot.*

Hindquarters—
The angulation of the hindquarters balances that of the forequarters. **(a)** *Hind legs* straight and parallel when viewed from the rear. Muscular with width in the region of the stifles which are well bent; femur and tibia are about equal in length; hock to heel short and perpendicular to the ground. When standing, the rear toes are only slightly behind the point of the rump. *Major fault: Cow-hocks.*

Coat—
(a)*Quality*— (1) Curly: of naturally harsh texture, dense throughout. (2) Corded: hanging

JOHN R. QUINN

Front view of a well-knit foot compared to a splay foot. Splay feet are considered a major fault in the Poodle.

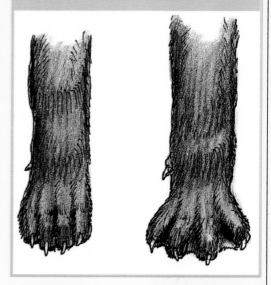

is permissible. *(2)"**English Saddle**":* In the "English Saddle" clip, the face, throat, feet, forelegs and base of the tail are shaved, leaving puffs on the forelegs and a pompon on the end of the tail. The hindquarters are covered with a short blanket of hair except for a curved shaved area on each flank and two shaved bands on each hind leg. The entire shaven foot and a portion of the shaven leg above the puff are visible. The rest of the body is left in full coat but may be shaped in order to insure overall balance. *(4) "**Sporting**":* In the "Sporting" clip, a Poodle shall be shown with face, feet, throat, and base of tail shaved, leaving a scissored cap on the top of the head and a pompon on the end of the tail. The rest of the body and legs are clipped or scissored to follow the outline of the dog, leaving a short blanket of coat no longer than one inch in length. The hair on the legs may be slightly longer than that on the body.

In all clips the hair of the topknot may be left free or held in place by elastic bands. The hair is only of sufficient length to present a smooth outline. "Topknot" refers only to hair on the skull, from stop to occiput. This is the only area where elastic bands may be used.

Color— The coat is an even and solid color at the skin. In blues, grays, silvers, browns, cafe-au-laits, apricots and creams, the coat may show varying shades of the same color. This is frequently present in the somewhat darker feathering of the ears and in the tipping of the ruff. While clear

JOHN R. QUINN

In the Lion or "English Saddle" clip, the face, throat, feet, forelegs, and base of the tail are shaved, leaving puffs on the forelegs and a pompon on the end of the tail.

colors are definitely preferred, such natural variation in the shading of the coat is not to be considered a fault. Brown and cafe-au-lait Poodles have liver-colored noses, eye rims and lips, dark toenails and dark amber eyes. Black, blue, gray, silver, cream and white Poodles have black noses, eye rims and lips, black or self colored toenails and very dark eyes. In the apricots, while the foregoing coloring is preferred, liver-colored noses, eye rims and lips, and amber eyes are permitted but are not desirable.
Major faults: Color of nose, lips

and eye rims incomplete, or of wrong color for color of dog.

Parti-colored dogs shall be *disqualified.* The coat of a parti-colored dog is not an even solid color at the skin but is of two or more colors.

Gait—

A straightforward trot with light springy action and strong hindquarters drive. Head and tail carried up. Sound effortless movement is essential.

Temperament—

Carrying himself proudly, very active, intelligent, the Poodle has about him an air of distinction

The desired gait is a straightforward trot with light springy action and strong drive from the rear. This black Standard Poodle is showing off his excellent gait at an outdoor dog show.

ISABELLE FRANCAIS

Color in the Poodle is never an important consideration, provided that the color is solid and even. These three Poodles are black, white and cafe au lait.

and dignity peculiar to himself. *Major faults: Shyness or sharpness.*

Major Faults— Any distinct deviation from the desired characteristics described in the Breed Standard.

Disqualifications Size—*A dog over or under the height limits specified shall be disqualified.* **Clip—***A dog in any type of clip other than those listed under Coat shall be disqualified.* **Parti-colors—** *The coat of a parti-color dog is not an even solid color at the skin but of two or more colors. Parti-color dogs shall be disqualified.*

A parti-color Poodle is disqualified from the show ring according to the breed standard. Despite this fact, many people enjoy the novelty and attractive appearance of the parti-color or harlequin Poodle.

ISABELLE FRANCAIS

THE KENNEL CLUB (GREAT BRITAIN) VARIATIONS

Head and Skull: Long and fine with slight peak at the back. The skull not broad and with a moderate stop. Foreface strong and well chiseled, not falling away under the eyes.

Coat: It is strongly recommended that the traditional lion clip "English Saddle clip" in the United States) be adhered to.

Size: *Standard—*15 inches (38cm) and over. *Miniature—*Height at shoulder should be under 15 inches (38 cm) but not under 11 inches (28 cm). *Toy—*Height at shoulder should be under 11 inches (28 cm).

GROOMING YOUR POODLE

Every self-respecting Poodle must be clipped and groomed. Unless he is reasonably well kept, a Poodle is unhappy and very uncomfortable. In fact, to neglect a Poodle's coat is to be cruel to him.

in turn causes him to tear his hair out so that he gets bald patches and sores. If you plan to buy a Poodle, or if you already own one, make it a point to keep him well-groomed and have him clipped at regular intervals. If you

ISABELLE FRANCAIS

Poodle people accept the fact that their dogs require more grooming than any other breed of dog. To keep Poodles looking their best, an owner must learn the ropes of grooming or make regular visits to a grooming salon.

THE POODLE'S COAT

A Poodle's coat is very thick and doesn't shed in the ordinary way. The old hair tangles up in the new and mats down. In hot weather this makes the dog feel the heat even more than usual. The dirt and dust gradually work down to the skin and set up irritation, causing the dog to scratch. This

neglect his coat and general appearance, your Poodle will suffer.

For perfection, a Poodle should have a daily grooming, but if this is impossible, then be sure that he is groomed at least twice a week. This will mean that your dog's coat will be in reasonably good condition.

If a Poodle is left out in the rain often, or if you live in a very damp climate, remember that getting the coat wet constantly means that it will tangle and mat down. Towel the dog well when you bring him in and if you have an electric hand-held drier, dry him carefully, especially before putting him to bed. Philip Howard-Price, the well-known English breeder, and owner of the famous Montfleuri kennels, lost his beloved and very beautiful bitch, Trilla of Montfleuri, because a careless kennel-maid didn't bother to dry her when she came in wet from a walk. Trilla got pneumonia and died—a most beautiful bitch and a terrible loss to the breed. Take a lesson from this, and don't let your Poodle go to bed wet. However, don't let this alarm you. Poodles are really a very healthy breed. All they

Putting the finishing touches on this gorgeous Standard Poodle before entering the show ring.

require is good food, good grooming, and common sense in caring for them.

EQUIPMENT

The best brush for a Poodle's coat is a pin-bristled brush. The bristles are set fairly wide apart on a rubber base, and are straight, not curved. The wide-apart, curved bristles aren't good for the coat. You will also need a small slicker brush.

These and other supplies can be purchased at your local pet shop. You will require two combs, one coarse-toothed steel comb, with or without a handle, and a fine comb. These few items and, of course, a small animal clipper and a good pair of barber's shears are all you will require to keep your Poodle's coat in tip-top condition. Coat dressing or oils are useful, if you want to do a really good job of grooming.

GROOMING TRAINING

Whether your dog is a show dog or a house pet, there is only one way to teach him to be groomed so that the job is easily accomplished and satisfactorily done, and that is to lay him on his side!

Take him and lay him down gently on his side on the table or you. You should be able to take his paws and turn him over onto his other side without any trouble at all.

HOW TO GROOM

How you groom and care for a Poodle's coat is the secret of how good your dog is going to look. A scruffy-looking coat can spoil the most beautiful Poodle that ever walked, just as a correctly groomed coat can make a

A menagerie of coat care products are needed for Poodle maintenance and can be purchased at pet shops or pet supply houses.

wherever you expect will be the usual place to groom him. If his head comes up, push it firmly down and say "stay!" as you do so. If he kicks and struggles, say the same thing and push him down again, and keep pushing him down. When you have pushed him down firmly a few times, he will begin to get the idea, and by the second or third time you groom him, you will find that your dog will lie quietly for

mediocre Poodle look a hundred percent better than he really is. Here is how it is done.

Have your Poodle lying on his side, relaxed and quiet. Take your steel-bristled brush and part a section of the coat, starting either up along the spine or down along the brisket. For argument's sake, say you are starting up on the spine. Part the hair with the brush. Using gentle, firm, slow strokes, brush the hair away from

Grooming salons offer excellent and convenient services. When trained at home to accept the grooming procedure, Poodles make polite and patient patrons.

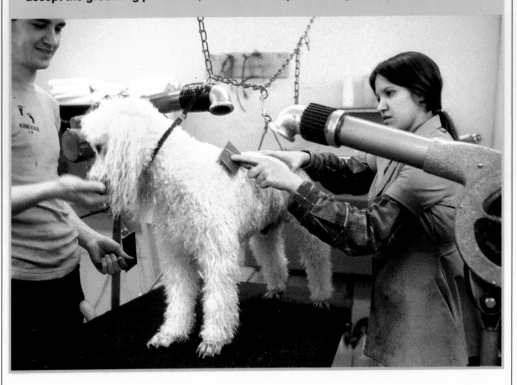

The process of grooming a Poodle to perfection is fairly intricate and involves many steps. Depending on the clip you choose for your Poodle, the steps will vary, as a Puppy Clip is less time consuming than a Lion or "English Saddle" clip.

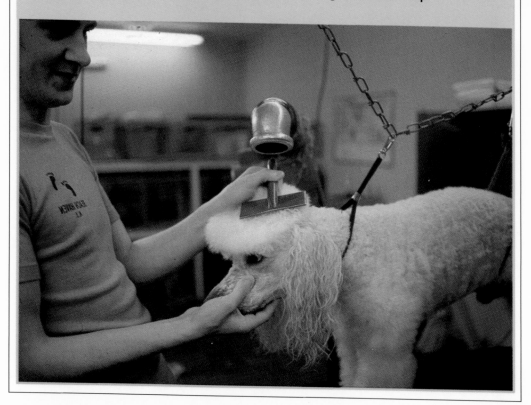

you and away from the spine. Then, taking your wide-toothed comb, work very gently along where you have brushed. Take care not to tear out any live hairs. When you have done this all along the parted section of coat, take your brush and part the hair again about half an inch from the first parting, and brush that gently and smoothly away from you, and then comb it. Do this all down one side of your dog; then, taking the dog by his feet, turn him gently over onto the other side and repeat the same performance there. When you have finished the second side,

Beginners with Poodles can benefit from an all-around grooming kit that provides all the essentials needed to clip their dog. Photograph courtesy of Wahl Clipper.

Grooming aids such as bath oils and conditioners can add to your Poodle's finished coat quality. Photograph courtesy of Hagen.

stand the dog up and (starting down near the elbows) part the chest hair in the same way, and brush and comb that all out as you did the sides. Then do the topknot with brush and comb in the same manner, and finally the ears and tail.

In describing how to brush and comb a Poodle, I have told you to groom the sides, chest, etc. In this, I had in mind the show clip, hence there is no mention of the legs. Brush the leg furnishings just as you would the show dog's ruff, and your Poodle will always look immaculate.

GROOMING AIDS

Many professional handlers tell you to spray your Poodle's coat with coat dressing or coat oil before you start grooming. With a show dog, this procedure is imperative in order that the tips of the hairs are not broken; but with a pet Poodle, where great length of coat is unimportant, one can safely groom the coat without the aid of any sprays or oils. However, if your dog's coat has become matted in the rain, or if he has been swimming in the ocean, or something of that sort, then your pet will benefit considerably from the use of oils or coat dressings, more particularly from oil. Excessive dampness or long immersion in water dries out the natural oils in the coat and renders it dull-looking and dry—and very prone to breaking off in patches. This, of course, can spoil the best-looking clip, for to look nice the coat must, of course, be in good condition.

There are a variety of products on the market which are good for Poodle coats. Go into your nearest pet shop and you will be advised on the various types.

ISABELLE FRANCAIS

Always brush out a Poodle before bath time. This avoids making any existing mats worse. This young Miniature Poodle seems fairly content in his bath.

BATHING

Next is your Poodle's bath. Remember, before bathing a Poodle, he must always be brushed and combed as described here—before you put him in the bath. If you bathe an unbrushed, uncombed Poodle, all you do is wet the mats so that it is almost impossible to get them out, and you can't get the dog really clean, because all the dirt and dust inside those mats is left there. When—and if—you can get those mats out, every place where they were will have a little dusty, dirty patch. This, of course, will spoil the appearance of the most beautiful coat, and this is to be avoided.

Having brushed the dog thoroughly and combed out all the mats, you are now ready to bathe him. Have two or three towels on hand for when you lift him out of the laundry-tray or tub. Have a hand-held dryer where you can get at it easily, and your shampoo ready mixed, preferably in an unbreakable container. If you are going to use something for fleas,

Rinse all the soap out of the coat. Be thorough and careful so as to avoid any skin irritations developing from soap residue left in the coat.

have that ready also.

Before we go any further, a word of advice on shampoos! A dog's skin is as delicate as a baby's. Indeed, some people say it's more delicate than that. However, the point is that you just can't use any soap or shampoo for a Poodle, because if you do, the coat will not be in good condition. Many Poodles, particularly whites and light-colored ones, will get severe skin irritation if bathed with an unsuitable soap or shampoo.

When you go to your nearest pet shop to buy your grooming equipment and clippers, get a good quality dog shampoo as well. There are many excellent ones, some made especially for Poodles. For silvers there is an excellent creamy shampoo that gives a really wonderful glint to a silver's coat. For whites there is a bluish colored shampoo that gives a wonderful finish, and another for browns that is very good. The best results for blacks can be had with an ordinary liquid dog shampoo. This seems to really bring out the jet-black gleam of the coat and sets the dog off to perfection.

Run the water and get the temperature adjusted before putting your dog in the tub. This is important, for dogs cannot stand water as hot as humans can, so fix it just medium warm, and see how your dog likes it. If it seems too chilly for him, increase the amount of hot water. It is a good idea, before you wet him, to put a little baby oil in his eyes if the shampoo you are using is at all likely to irritate them. However, most dog shampoos do not irritate the eyes, as they are especially made for dogs. If you are afraid of getting water in the ears, put a little ball of cotton in each. Some dogs, of course, just won't go for this at all, and go nearly frantic when you put it in, pawing and scratching at their ears until they get it out. If you are careful in your shampooing, the likelihood of getting any water in the ears is slight. Never wash inside a dog's ears. This is definitely harmful and can lead to ear trouble later on. Poodles are a very healthy breed, but their one weakness is their ears, and they can be subject to ear trouble.

ISABELLE FRANCAIS

Before towel drying the dog, squeeze out as much water as possible. Blot him dry with a towel and warm him up before beginning any further grooming. Any dampness in the coat will cause the coat to curl up from the roots.

Having gotten the dog thoroughly wet, pour some shampoo down the back and work up a good lather. Then go down the legs—not forgetting the feet—and then do the tail and finally the head and ears. When the whole dog is fully lathered, rinse him off and lather a second time. Give a very thorough final rinsing and then pour a little flea solution down his back and a little on the underside, taking care not to put it on the male dog's testicles or penis, as it can irritate these organs.

When you have finished bathing your Poodle, squeeze as much water out of the coat as you can before you lift him back on the grooming table. (This helps considerably in short-ening the drying period.) Then wrap him up in towels and blot him off a little, and finally give him a brisk rub. This will warm him and dry up quite a lot of excess water. Now, turn on your dryer and begin to dry him.

There's not much use in brushing him until most of the dampness has gone, but as soon as you can, set to work with your brush, and brush him dry. If you have a crate with a dryer that blows into it, then you can leave the dog in there until he is dry, and then take your Poodle out and brush him. However, you can't do this with a show dog.

Make quite sure that your Poodle is really dry before you take him off the grooming table. If you don't get him dry right down to the skin, in just a few hours his hair will have curled up for about an inch from the roots of his hair, and no matter how carefully you groom him afterwards you just can't get those tight little curls out at the base of the coat, and the whole appearance of your finished clip will be spoiled.

ISABELLE FRANCAIS

Once the dog is thoroughly dry, you can brush him out and spend some time admiring his new "do".

YOUR POODLE'S HEALTH

We know our pets, their moods and habits, and therefore we can recognize when our Poodle is experiencing an off-day. Signs of sickness can be very obvious or very subtle. As any mother can attest, diagnosing and treating an ailment require common sense, knowing when to seek home remedies and when to visit your doctor...or veterinarian, as the case may be.

Your veterinarian, we know, is your Poodle's best friend, next to you. It will pay to be choosy about your veterinarian. Talk to dog-owning friends whom you respect. Visit more than one vet before you make a lifelong choice. Trust your instincts. Find a knowledgeable, compassionate vet who knows Poodles and likes them.

ISABELLE FRANCAIS

Poodles are mellow but attentive: know your Poodle's moods so that you recognize when he's not feeling his best.

Grooming for good health makes good sense. Always check your Poodle's coat for parasites or foreign objects. The thick coat helps to protect the dog, but also can hide bugs and such from the naked eye. Most Poodles love to be brushed and groomed. Brushing stimulates the natural oils in the coat and also removes dead haircoat.

Anal sacs, sometimes called anal glands, are located in the

musculature of the anal ring, one on either side. Each empties into the rectum via a small duct. Occasionally their secretion becomes thickened and accumulates so you can readily feel these structures from the outside. If your Poodle is scooting across the floor dragging his rear quarters, or licking his rear, his anal sacs may need to be expressed. Placing pressure in

plague many Poodles due to their long ears and heavy tufts. Bathing the ear in a solution of half-hydrogen peroxide and water can help prevent recurrent infections. Always dry the ear well. Since ear infections can sometimes lead to partial or complete loss of hearing, consult a veterinarian with any persistent cases.

The Poodle's coat and skin can be prone to atopic dermatitis,

ISABELLE FRANCAIS

The Poodle's skin and coat can be very sensitive. Some dogs are allergic to grasses and weeds, so be sure to tell your veterinarian that your itchy Poodle spends a lot of time outdoors. Owner, Maryann K. Howarth.

and up toward the anus, while holding the tail, is the general routine. Anal sac secretions are characteristically foul-smelling, and you could get squirted if not careful. Veterinarians can take care of this during regular visits and demonstrate the cleanest method.

The most common health concerns of Poodles center on the eyes, ears and skin. Ear infections

inherited sebaceous adenitis and seborrhea. When grooming your Poodle, check for possible growths, tumors, or unidentified marks. Better thorough than sorry. The very dense coat of this unique breed of dog deserves regular attention to keep healthy and clean.

Eye abnormalities include cataracts, rod-cone degeneration, occurring at three to five years, and PRA, an inherited defect that can severely reduce a dog's vision. Screening for eye problems has therefore been prioritized in this breed as well as countless others.

Poodles can be predisposed to certain other congenital and inherited abnormalities, such as hip dysplasia, a blatantly common problem in purebred dogs with few exceptions. HD affects Standard Poodles more commonly than either the Miniature or Toy. New owners must insist on screening certificates from such hip registries as OFA or PennHIP. Since HD is hereditary, it's necessary to know that the parents and grandparents of your puppy had hips rated good or better. Dysplastic dogs suffer from badly constructed hip joints that become arthritic and very painful, thereby hindering the dog's ability to be a working dog, a good-moving show dog, or even a happy, active pet.

Elbow dysplasia has recently become more of a concern, and the OFA screens for elbows as well. Young dogs typically show signs of limping or rotating elbows when walking or running, which may indicate that elbow dysplasia is present.

Von Willebrand's disease, a bleeding disorder, and Legg-Perthes, kidney stones, and achondroplasia are conditions

ISABELLE FRANCAIS

Eye problems in Poodles are not uncommon. If you plan to breed your dog, have his eyes screened for any abnormalities so as to not pass a defect on.

that affect the Poodle and have been reported by veterinarians in recent times.

Epilepsy, a possible hereditary condition that is linked to the brain's receiving incorrect stimulus, hinders many breeds of dog and is problematic in Poodles. Affected dogs show signs of mild seizures between six months and three years. Although uncurable, fits can be treated with medication. A similar disorder, amaurotic idiocy, also occurs in Poodles but is not common.

Hypothyroidism (malfunction of the thyroid gland) can be linked to many symptoms in Standard Poodles, such as obesity, lethargy, and reproductive disorders. Supplementation of the thyroid decreases problems, though such dogs should likely not be bred.

Toy Poodles are prone to hypoglycemia (abnormal decrease in blood sugar), though this is usually an easily managed situation of which most qualified veterinarians are aware.

Despite this lengthy list of potential problems, a well-bred Poodle is a healthy, long-lived companion animal. Proper care and education can only help owners promote the health and longevity of their dogs. Most

ISABELLE FRANCAIS

Many complicated health problems in the Poodle, and dogs in general, manifest themselves in very ordinary ways: lethargy, obesity, lack of appetite. Always consult your vet whenever your Poodle isn't acting like himself.

Poodles are among the longest lived of dogs. They are naturally hardy and physically and mentally sound, often living to twenty years of age.

breeders advise against feeding the Standard Poodle one large meal per day because of the dangers of bloat (gastric torsion): the twisting of the stomach causes gas to build up and the organ expands like a balloon. Avoiding strenuous exercise and large amounts of water can preclude the occurrence of bloat, as can feeding two smaller meals instead of one larger one. A good commercial dog food is recommended for the dog's balanced diet.

For the continued health of your dog, owners must attend to vaccinations regularly. Your veterinarian can recommend a vaccination schedule appropriate for your dog, taking into consideration the factors of climate and geography. The basic vaccinations to protect your dog are: parvovirus, distemper, hepatitis, leptospirosis, adenovirus, parainfluenza, coronavirus, bordetella, tracheobronchitis (kennel cough), Lyme disease and rabies.

Parvovirus a is highly contagious, dog-specific disease, first recognized in 1978. Targeting the small intestine, parvo affects the stomach, and diarrhea and vomiting (with blood) are clinical signs. Although the dog can pass the infection to other dogs within

ISABELLE FRANCAIS

Poodles require a moderate amount of exercise. Never allow your Poodle to run vigorous after he has eaten. Such safe practices as this guards against upset stomachs and, more importantly, bloat.

three days of infection, the initial signs, which include lethargy and depression, don't display themselves until four to seven days. When affecting puppies under four weeks of age, the heart muscle is frequently attacked. When the heart is affected, the puppies exhibit difficulty in breathing and experience crying and foaming at the nose and

from the distemper infection. Such dogs experience seizures, general weakness and rigidity, as well as "hardpad." Since distemper is largely incurable, prevention through vaccination is vitally important. Puppies should be vaccinated at six to eight weeks of age, with boosters at ten to 12 weeks. Older puppies (16 weeks and older) who are

ROBERT PEARCY

Before entering your Poodle in a local obedience class, be sure he has been properly vaccinated. Many canine maladies can be passed from dog to dog so it makes sense to protect your dog by vaccinating him.

mouth.

Distemper, related to human measles, is an airborne virus that spreads in the blood and ultimately in the nervous system and epithelial tissues. Young dogs or dogs with weak immune systems can develop encephalomyelitis (brain disease)

unvaccinated should receive no fewer than two vaccinations at three- to four-week intervals.

Hepatitis mainly affects the liver and is caused by canine adenovirus type I. Highly infectious, hepatitis often affects dogs nine to 12 months of age. Initially the virus localizes in the

ISABELLE FRANCAIS

Certain dog diseases can be passed to humans as well. Vaccinating your dog protects him and you from potential illness.

spread leptospirosis enter through the mucous membranes and spread to the internal organs via the bloodstream. It can be passed through the dog's urine. Leptospirosis does not affect young dogs as consistently as do the other viruses; it is reportedly regional in distribution and somewhat dependent on the immunostatus of the dog. Fever, inappetence, vomiting, dehydration, hemorrhage, kidney and eye disease can result in moderate cases.

Bordetella, called canine cough, causes a persistent hacking cough in dogs and is very contagious. Bordetella involves a virus and a bacteria: parainfluenza is the most common virus implicated; *Bordetella bronchiseptica*, the bacterium. Bronchitis and pneumonia result in less than 20 percent of the cases, and most dogs recover from the condition

ROBERT SMITH

Miniature Poodle posing: the picture of health.

dog's tonsils and then disperses to the liver, kidney and eyes. Generally speaking the dog's immune system is capable of combating this virus. Canine infectious hepatitis affects dogs whose systems cannot fight off the adenovirus. Affected dogs have fever, abdominal pains, bruising on mucous membranes and gums, and experience coma and convulsions. Prevention of hepatitis exists only through vaccination at eight to ten weeks of age and then boosters three or four weeks later, then annually.

Leptospirosis is a bacterium-related disease, often spread by rodents. The organisms that within a week to four weeks. Non-prescription medicines can help relieve the hacking cough, though nothing can cure the condition before it's run its course. Vaccination cannot guarantee protection from canine cough, but it does ward off the most common virus responsible for the condition.

Lyme disease (also called borreliosis), although known for decades, was only first diagnosed in dogs in 1984. Lyme disease can affect cats, cattle, and horses, but especially people. In the U.S., the disease is transmitted by two ticks carrying the *Borrelia burgdorferi* organism: the deer tick (*Ixodes scapularis*) and the western black-legged tick (*Ixodes pacificus*), the latter primarily affects reptiles. In Europe, *Ixodes ricinus* is responsible for

ISABELLE FRANCAIS

Although many dogs love the beach and ocean, dangers lurk in this inviting environment: fungal infections from the sand, such as ringworm, fleas and ticks in grassy dunes and possible overexposure to the sun.

spreading Lyme. The disease causes lameness, fever, joint swelling, inappetence, and lethargy. Removal of ticks from the dog's coat can help reduce the chances of Lyme, though not as much as avoiding heavily wooded areas where the dog is most likely to contract ticks. A vaccination is available, though it has not been proven to protect dogs from all strains of the organism that causes the disease.

Rabies is passed to dogs and people through wildlife: in North America, principally through the skunk, fox and raccoon; the bat is not the culprit it was once thought to be. Likewise, the common image of the rabid dog foaming at the mouth with every hair on end is unlikely the truest scenario. A rabid dog exhibits difficulty eating, salivates much and has spells of paralysis and awkwardness. Before a dog reaches this final state, it may experience anxiety, personality changes, irritability and more aggressiveness than is usual. Some reports show that Poodles are sensitive to the rabies vaccination—please discuss this possibility with your vet. If safe, vaccinations are of course recommended as rabid dogs are too dangerous to manage and are commonly euthanized. Puppies are generally vaccinated at 12 weeks of age, and then annually. Although rabies is on the decline in the world community, tens of thousands of humans die each year from rabies-related incidents.

Parasites have clung to our pets for centuries. Despite our modern efforts, fleas still pester our pet's existence, and our own. All dogs itch, and fleas can make even the happiest dog a miserable, scabby mess. The loss of hair and habitual biting and chewing at themselves rank among the annoyances; the nuisances include the passing of tapeworms and the whole family's itching through the summer months. A full range of flea-control and elimination products are available at pet shops, and your veterinarian surely has recommendations. Sprays, powders, collars and dips fight fleas from the outside; drops and pills fight the good fight from inside. Discuss the possibilities with your vet. Not all products can be used in conjunction with one another, and some dogs may be more sensitive to certain applications than others. The dog's living quarters must be debugged as well as the dog itself. Heavy infestation may require multiple treatments.

Always check your dog for ticks carefully. Although fleas can be acquired almost anywhere, ticks

ROBERT SMITH

Poodles outdoors are prone to pick up parasites. Always check your dog carefully after you've been in the park or another grassy, wooded area.

Unless attended to, fleas are for keeps. An itchy Poodle is an unhappy Poodle: many effective flea preparations are available at pet shops and can bring your dog relief.

are more likely to be picked up in heavy treed areas, pastures or other outside grounds (such as dog shows or obedience or field trials). Athletic, active, and hunting dogs are the most likely subjects, though any passing dog can be the host. Remember Lyme disease is passed by tick infestation.

As for internal parasites, worms are potentially dangerous for dogs and people. Roundworms, hookworms, whipworms, tapeworms, and heartworms comprise the blightsome party of troublemakers. Deworming puppies begins at around two to three weeks and continues until three months of age. Proper hygienic care of the environment is also important to prevent contamination with roundworm and hookworm eggs. Heartworm preventatives are recommended by most veterinarians, although there are some drawbacks to the regular introduction of poisons into our dogs' systems. These daily or monthly preparations also help regulate most other worms as well. Discuss worming procedures with your veterinarian.

Roundworms pose a great threat to dogs and people. They are found in the intestine of dogs and can be passed to people through ingestion of feces-contaminated dirt. Roundworm infection can be prevented by not walking dogs in heavy-traffic people areas, by burning feces, and by curbing dogs in a responsible manner. (Of course, in most areas of the country, curbing dogs is the law.) Roundworms are typically passed from the bitch to the litter, and bitches should be treated along with the puppies, even if she tested negative prior to whelping. Generally puppies are treated every two weeks until two months of age.

Hookworms, like roundworms, are also a danger to dogs and people. The hookworm parasite (known as *Ancylostoma caninum*) causes cutaneous larva migrans in people. The eggs of hookworms are passed in feces and become infective in shady, sandy areas. The larvae penetrate the skin of the dog, and the dog subsequently becomes infected. When swallowed, these parasites affect the intestines, lungs, windpipe,

ROBERT SMITH

Even standing tall in the grass, you still won't avoid those hopping pesty parasites!

and the whole digestive system. Infected dogs suffer from anemia and lose large amounts of blood in the places where the worms latch onto the dog's intestines, etc.

Although infrequently passed to humans, whipworms are cited as one of the most common parasites in America. These elongated worms affect the intestines of the dog, where they latch on, and cause colic upset or diarrhea. Unless identified in stools passed, whipworms are difficult to diagnose. Adult worms can be eliminated more consistently than the larvae, since whipworms exhibit unusual life cycles. Proper hygienic care of outdoor grounds is critical to the avoidance of these harmful parasites.

Tapeworms are carried by fleas, and enter the dog when the dog swallows the flea. Humans can acquire tapeworms in the same way, though we are less likely to swallow fleas than dogs are. Recent studies have shown that certain rodents and other wild animals have been infected with tapeworms, and dogs can be affected by catching and/ or eating these other animals. Of course, outdoor hunting dogs and terriers are more likely to be infected in this way than are your typical house dog or non-motivated hound. Treatment for tapeworm has proven very effective, and infected dogs do not show great discomfort or symptoms. When people are infected, however, the liver can be seriously damaged. Proper cleanliness is the best bet against tapeworms.

Heartworm disease is transmitted by mosquitoes and badly affects the lungs, heart and blood vessels of dogs. The larvae of *Dirofilaria immitis* enters the dog's bloodstream when bitten by an infected mosquito. The larvae takes about six months to mature. Infected dogs suffer from weight loss, appetite loss, chronic coughing and general fatigue. Not all affected dogs show signs of illness right away, and carrier dogs may be affected for years before clinical signs appear. Treatment of heartworm disease has been effective but can be dangerous also. Prevention as always is the desirable alternative. Ivermectin is the active ingredient in most heartworm preventatives and has proven to be successful. Check with your veterinarian for the preparation best for your dog. Dogs generally begin taking the preventatives at eight months of age and continue to do so throughout the non-winter months.

Heartworm preparations protect our dogs from possible infection from mosquitoes, which carry the heartworm larvae.

YOUR NEW POODLE PUPPY

SELECTION

When you do pick out a Poodle puppy as a pet, don't be hasty; the longer you study puppies, the better you will understand them. Make it your transcendent concern to select only one that radiates good health and spirit and is lively on his feet, whose eyes are bright, whose coat shines, and who comes forward eagerly to make and to cultivate your acquaintance. Don't fall for any shy little darling that wants to retreat to his bed or his box, or plays coy behind other puppies or people, or hides his head under your arm or jacket appealing to your protective instinct. *Pick the Poodle puppy who forthrightly picks you! The feeling of attraction should be mutual!*

ISABELLE FRANCAIS

Poodles come in more colors than most other dog breeds. Don't prejudge a puppy by its color: it is the least important of all factors.

DOCUMENTS

Now, a little paper work is in order. When you purchase a purebred Poodle puppy, you should receive a transfer of ownership, registration material, and other "papers" (a list of the immunization shots, if any, the puppy may have been given; a note on whether or not the puppy has been wormed; a diet and feeding schedule to which the puppy is accustomed) and you are welcomed as a fellow owner to a long, pleasant association with a most lovable pet, and more (news)paper work.

GENERAL PREPARATION

You have chosen to own a particular Poodle puppy. You have chosen it very carefully over all other breeds and all other puppies. So before you ever get that Poodle puppy home, you will have prepared for its arrival by reading everything you can get your hands on having to do with the management of Poodles and puppies. True, you will run into many conflicting opinions, but at least you will not be starting "blind." Read, study, digest. Talk over your plans with your veterinarian, other "Poodle people," and the seller of your Poodle puppy.

Two tiny Toy Poodle puppies ready to go home.

When you get your Poodle puppy, you will find that your reading and study are far from finished. You've just scratched the surface in your plan to provide the greatest possible comfort and health for your Poodle; and, by

Personalities in a litter begin to be apparent at a very young age, even though the puppies may seem identical in every other regard.

the same token, you do want to assure yourself of the greatest possible enjoyment of this wonderful creature. You must be ready for this puppy mentally as well as in the physical requirements.

TRANSPORTATION

If you take the puppy home by car, protect him from drafts, particularly in cold weather. Wrapped in a towel and carried in the arms or lap of a passenger, the Poodle puppy will usually make the trip without mishap. If the pup starts to drool and to squirm, stop the car for a few minutes. Have newspapers handy in case of car-sickness. A covered carton lined with newspapers provides protection for puppy and

ISABELLE FRANCAIS

Because Poodles come in three varieties—and so many colors— knowing you want a Poodle is only half the decision.

ISABELLE FRANCAIS

The Toy Poodle is the handiest: less Poodle to groom and feed, but no less to love.

car, if you are driving alone. Avoid excitement and unnecessary handling of the puppy on arrival. A Poodle puppy is a very small "package" to be making a complete change of surroundings and company, and he needs frequent rest and refreshment to renew his vitality.

THE FIRST DAY AND NIGHT

When your Poodle puppy arrives in your home, put him down on the floor and don't pick him up again, except when it is absolutely necessary. He is a dog, a real dog, and must not be lugged around like a rag doll. Handle him as little as possible, and permit no one to pick him up and baby him. To repeat, *put your Poodle puppy on the floor or the ground and let him stay there except when it may be necessary to do otherwise.*

Quite possibly your Poodle lights. Let him roam for a few minutes while you and everyone else concerned sit quietly or go about your routine business. Let the puppy come back to you.

Playmates may cause an immediate problem if the new Poodle puppy is to be greeted by children or other pets. If not, you

ISABELLE FRANCAIS

Puppies inherit their parents' looks and, to a lesser extent, their personalities as well. It's fun but important to meet the parents of your puppy to get an idea how he'll look and how he'll act.

puppy will be afraid for a while in his new surroundings, without his mother and littermates. Comfort him and reassure him, but don't console him. Don't give him the "oh-you-poor-itsy-bitsy-puppy" treatment. Be calm, friendly, and reassuring. Encourage him to walk around and sniff over his new home. If it's dark, put on the can skip this subject. The natural affinity between puppies and children calls for some supervision until a live-and-let-live relationship is established. This applies particularly to a Christmas puppy, when there is more excitement than usual and more chance for a puppy to swallow something upsetting. It is a better plan to welcome the puppy several days before or after the holiday week. Like a baby, your Poodle puppy needs much rest and should not be over-handled. Once a child realizes that a puppy has "feelings" similar to his own, and can readily be hurt or injured, the opportunities for play and responsibilities provide exercise and training for both.

For his first night with you, he should be put where he is to sleep every night—say in the kitchen, since its floor can usually be easily cleaned. Let him explore the kitchen to his heart's content; close doors to confine him there. Prepare his food and feed him lightly the first night. Give him a pan with some water in it—not a lot, since most puppies will try to drink the whole pan dry. Give him an old coat or shirt to lie on. Since a coat or shirt will be strong in human scent, he will pick it out to lie on, thus furthering his feeling of security in the room where he has just been fed.

Hopefully your Poodle's breeder will have instilled the basics of housebreaking during the weaning and socialization period. Dogs are naturally clean animals, and housebreaking is but a natural extension of good instincts.

FEEDING

Now let's talk about feeding your Poodle, a subject so simple that it's amazing there is so much nonsense and misunderstanding about it. Is it expensive to feed a Poodle? No, it is not! You can feed your Poodle economically and keep him in perfect shape the

they become accustomed to. Many dogs flatly refuse to eat nice, fresh beef. They pick around it and eat everything else. But meat—bah! Why? They aren't accustomed to it! They'd eat rabbit fast enough, but they refuse beef because they aren't used to it.

ISABELLE FRANCAIS

Poodles can be picky eaters. Avoid spoiling your dog and you and he will be much happier in the long run.

year round, or you can feed him expensively. He'll thrive either way, and let's see why this is true.

First of all, remember a Poodle is a dog. Dogs do not have a high degree of selectivity in their food, and unless you spoil them with great variety (and possibly turn them into poor, "picky" eaters) they will eat almost anything that

VARIETY NOT NECESSARY

A good general rule of thumb is forget all human preferences and don't give a thought to variety. Choose the right diet for your Poodle and feed it to him day after day, year after year, winter and summer. But what is the right diet? Many breeders and owners don't agree.

Hundreds of thousands of dollars have been spent in canine nutrition research. The results are pretty conclusive, so you needn't go into a lot of experimenting with trials of this and that every other week. Research has proven just what your dog needs to eat and to keep healthy.

DOG FOOD

There are almost as many right diets as there are dog experts, but the basic diet most often recommended is one that consists of a dry food, either meal or kibble form. There are several of excellent quality, manufactured by reliable companies, research tested, and nationally advertised. They are inexpensive, highly satisfactory, and easily available in stores everywhere in containers of five to 50 pounds. Larger amounts cost less per pound, usually.

If you have a choice of brands, it is usually safer to choose the better known one; but even so, carefully read the analysis on the package. Do not choose any food in which the protein level is less than 25 percent, and be sure that this protein comes from both animal and vegetable sources. The good dog foods have meat meal, fish meal, liver, and such, plus protein from alfalfa and soy beans, as well as some dried-milk product. Note the vitamin content carefully. See that they are all there in good proportions; and be especially certain that the food contains properly high levels of vitamins A and D, two of the most perishable and important ones. Note the B-complex level, but don't worry about carbohydrate and mineral levels. These substances are plentiful and cheap and not likely to be lacking in a good brand.

ISABELLE FRANCAIS

Dry kibble is the choice of most Poodle breeders, though this alone is not enough to sustain a dog's 100 percent nutrition.

The advice given for how to choose a dry food also applies to moist or canned types of dog foods, if you decide to feed one of these.

Having chosen a really good

food, feed it to your Poodle as the manufacturer directs. And once you've started, stick to it. Never change if you can possibly help it. A switch from one meal or kibble-type food can usually be made without too much upset; however, a change will almost invariably give you (and your Poodle) some trouble.

WHEN SUPPLEMENTS ARE NEEDED

Now what about supplements of various kinds, mineral and vitamin, or the various oils? They are all okay to add to your Poodle's food. However, if you are feeding your Poodle a correct diet, and this is easy to do, no supplements are necessary unless your Poodle has been improperly fed, has been sick, or is having puppies. Vitamins and minerals are naturally present in all the foods; and to ensure against any loss through processing, they are added in concentrated form to the dog food you use. Except on the advice of your veterinarian, added amounts of vitamins can prove harmful to your Poodle! The same risk goes with minerals.

FEEDING SCHEDULE

When and how much food to give your Poodle? As to when (except in the instance of puppies), suit yourself. You may feed two meals per day or the same amount in one single feeding, either morning or night. As to how to prepare the food and how much to give, it is generally best to follow the directions on the food package. Your own Poodle may want a little more or a little less.

Fresh, cool water should

ISABELLE FRANCAIS

Rest time always follows meal time in the dog world. When the dogs are outdoors, be sure that fresh, cool water is available.

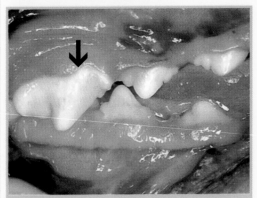

In a scientific study, this shows a dog's tooth (arrow) while being maintained by Gumabone chewing.

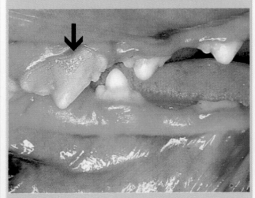

The Gumabone was taken away and in 30 days the tooth was almost completely covered with plaque and tarter.

gums, to ensure normal jaw development, and to settle the permanent teeth solidly in the jaws.

The adult Poodle's desire to chew stems from the instinct for tooth cleaning, gum massage, and jaw exercise—plus the need for an outlet for periodic doggie tensions.

This is why dogs, especially puppies and young dogs, will often destroy property worth hundreds of dollars when their chewing instinct is not diverted from their owner's possessions. And this is why you should provide your Poodle with

always be available to your Poodle. This is important to good health throughout his lifetime.

ALL POODLES NEED TO CHEW

Puppies and young Poodles need something with resistance to chew on while their teeth and jaws are developing—for cutting the puppy teeth, to induce growth of the permanent teeth under the puppy teeth, to assist in getting rid of the puppy teeth at the proper time, to help the permanent teeth through the

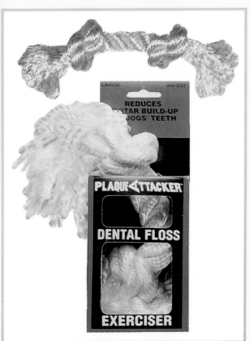

The nylon tug toy is actually a dental floss. You grab one end and let your Poodle tug on the other as it slowly slips through his teeth, since nylon is slippery. DO NOT use cotton rope tug toys as cotton will rot and tear into indigestable pieces which your dog will swallow.

something to chew—something that has the necessary functional qualities, is desirable from the Poodle's viewpoint, and is safe for him.

It is very important that your Poodle not be permitted to chew on anything he can break or on any indigestible thing from which he can bite sizable chunks. Sharp pieces, such as from a bone which can be broken by a dog, may pierce the intestinal wall and kill. Indigestible things that can be bitten off in chunks, such as from shoes or rubber or plastic toys, may cause an intestinal stoppage (if not regurgitated) and bring painful death, unless surgery is promptly performed.

Strong natural bones, such as 4- to 8-inch lengths of round shin bone from mature beef—either the kind you can get from a butcher or one of the variety available commercially in pet stores—may serve your Poodle's teething needs if his mouth is large enough to handle them effectively. You may be tempted to give your Poodle

Most pet shops have complete walls dedicated to safe pacifiers.

puppy a smaller bone and he may not be able to break it when you do, but puppies grow rapidly and the power of their jaws constantly increases until maturity. This means that a growing Poodle may break one of the smaller bones at any time, swallow the pieces, and die painfully before you realize what is wrong.

All hard natural bones are very abrasive. If your Poodle is an avid chewer, natural bones may wear away his teeth prematurely; hence, they then should be taken away from your dog when the teething purposes have been served. The badly worn, and usually painful, teeth of many mature dogs can be traced to excessive chewing on natural bones.

Contrary to popular belief, knuckle bones that can be chewed up and swallowed by your Poodle provide little, if any, usable calcium or other nutriment. They do, however, disturb the digestion of most dogs and cause them to vomit the nourishing food they need.

Dried rawhide products of various types, shapes, sizes, and prices are available on the market and have become quite popular. However, they don't serve the primary chewing functions very well; they are a bit messy when wet from mouthing, and most Poodles chew them up rather rapidly—but they have been considered safe for dogs until recently. Now, more and more incidents of death, and near death, by strangulation have been reported to be the results of partially swallowed chunks of rawhide swelling in the throat. More recently, some veterinarians have been attributing cases of acute constipation to large pieces of incompletely digested rawhide in the intestine.

A new product, molded rawhide, is very safe. During the process, the rawhide is melted and then injection molded into the familiar dog shape. It is very hard and is eagerly accepted by Poodles. The melting process also sterilizes the rawhide. Don't confuse this with pressed rawhide, which is nothing more than small strips of rawhide squeezed together.

The nylon bones, especially those with natural meat and bone fractions added, are probably the most complete, safe, and economical answer to the chewing need. Dogs cannot break them or bite off sizable chunks; hence, they are completely safe—and being longer lasting than other things offered for the purpose, they are economical.

Hard chewing raises little bristle-like projections on the surface of the nylon bones—to provide effective interim tooth cleaning and vigorous gum massage, much in the same way your toothbrush does it for you. The little projections are raked off and swallowed in the form of thin shavings, but the chemistry of the nylon is such that they break down in the stomach fluids and pass through without effect.

The toughness of the nylon provides the strong chewing resistance needed for important

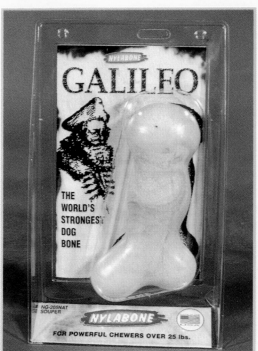

The Galileo is an extremely tough nylon pacifier. Its design is based upon original sketches by Galilieo. A book explaining the history and workings of the design come inside each package. This might very well be the best design for Poodles.

jaw exercise and effectively aids teething functions, but there is no tooth wear because nylon is non-abrasive. Being inert, nylon does not support the growth of micro-organisms; and it can be washed in soap and water or it can be sterilized by boiling or in an autoclave.

Nylabone® is highly reco-mmended by veterin-arians as a safe, healthy nylon bone that can't splinter or chip. Nylabone® is frizzled by the dog's chewing action, creating a toothbrush-like surface that cleanses the teeth and massages the gums. Nylabone®, the only chew products made of flavor-impregnated solid nylon, are available in your local pet shop. Nylabone® is superior to the cheaper bones because it is made of virgin nylon, which is the strongest and longest-lasting type of nylon available. The cheaper bones are made from recycled or re-ground nylon scraps, and have a tendency to break apart and split easily.

Nothing, however, substitutes for periodic professional attention for your Poodle's teeth and gums, not any more than your toothbrush can do

Take care of your Poodle's smile.

that for you. Have your Poodle's teeth cleaned at least once a year by your veterinarian (twice a year is better) and he will be happier, healthier, and far more pleasant to live with.

TRAINING

You owe proper training to your Poodle. The right and privilege of being trained is his birthright; and whether your Poodle is going to be a handsome, well-mannered housedog and companion, a show dog, or whatever possible use he may be put to, the basic training is always the same—all must start with basic obedience, or what might be called "manner training."

Your Poodle must come instantly when called and obey the "Sit" or "Down" command just as fast; he must walk quietly at "Heel," whether on or off lead. He must be mannerly and polite wherever he goes; he must be polite to strangers on the street and in stores. He must be mannerly in the presence of other dogs. He must not bark at children on roller skates, motorcycles, or other domestic animals. And he must be restrained from chasing cats. It is not a dog's inalienable right to chase cats, and he must be reprimanded for it.

PROFESSIONAL TRAINING

How do you go about this training? Well, it's a very simple procedure, pretty well standardized by now. First, if you can afford the extra expense, you may send your Poodle to a professional trainer, where in 30 to 60 days he will learn how to be a "good dog." If you enlist the services of a good professional trainer, follow his advice of when to come to see the dog. No, he won't forget you, but too-frequent visits at the wrong time may slow down his training progress. And using a "pro" trainer means that you will have to go for some training, too, after the trainer feels your Poodle is ready to go home. You will have to

ROBERT PEARCY

Hiring a professional trainer is a popular approach to dog training, though it doesn't necessarily guarantee that your well-trained dog will listen to you.

Hand signals are used in conjunction with voice commands. Your Poodle must learn to understand both.

Poodle's errors. Then, too, working with such a group, your Poodle will learn to get along with other dogs. And, what is more important, he will learn to do exactly what he is told to do, no matter how much confusion there is around him or how great the temptation is to go his own way.

Write to your national kennel club for the location of a training club or class in your locality. Sign up. Go to it regularly—every session! Go early and leave late! Both you and your Poodle will benefit tremendously.

TRAIN HIM BY THE BOOK

The third way of training your Poodle is by the book. Yes, you

Hiring a professional trainer is a popular approach to dog training, though it doesn't necessarily guarantee that your well-trained dog will listen to you.

learn how your Poodle works, just what to expect of him and how to use what the dog has learned after he is home.

OBEDIENCE TRAINING CLASS

Another way to train your Poodle (many experienced Poodle people think this is the best) is to join an obedience training class right in your own community. There is such a group in nearly every community nowadays. Here you will be working with a group of people who are also just starting out. You will actually be training your own dog, since all work is done under the direction of a head trainer who will make suggestions to you and also tell you when and how to correct your

CORINNE KAMER

can do it this way and do a good job of it too. But in using the book method, select a book, buy it, study it carefully; then study it some more, until the procedures are almost second nature to you. Then start your training. But stay with the book and its advice and exercises. Don't start in and then make up a few rules of your own. If you don't follow the book, you'll get into jams you can't get out of by yourself. If after a few hours of short training sessions your Poodle is still not working as he should, get back to the book for a study session, because it's your fault, not the dog's! The procedures of dog training have

Successful Dog Training is one of the better dog training books by Hollywood dog trainer Michael Kamer, who trains dogs for movie stars.

Poodle responding to hand signal to return to heel. Eventually the voice commands can be omitted and the dog will respond only to hand signals.

been so well systemized that it must be your fault, since literally thousands of fine Poodles have been trained by the book.

After your Poodle is "letter perfect" under all conditions, then, if you wish, go on to advanced training and trick work.

Your Poodle will love his obedience training, and you'll burst with pride at the finished product! Your Poodle will enjoy life even more, and you'll enjoy your Poodle more. And remember—you *owe good training to your Poodle.*

SHOWING YOUR POODLE

A show Poodle is a comparatively rare thing. He is one out of several litters of puppies. He happens to be born with a degree of physical perfection that closely approximates the standard by

animal. As a proven stud, he will automatically command a high price for service.

Showing Poodles is a lot of fun—yes, but it is a highly competitive sport. While all the experts were once beginners, the

ROBERT PEARCY

Poodles can begin their show careers as early as three months of age. This young pup is being reviewed on the table by the judge.

which the breed is judged in the show ring. Such a dog should, on maturity, be able to win or approach his championship in good, fast company at the larger shows. Upon finishing his championship, he is apt to be as highly desirable as a breeding

odds are against a novice. You will be showing against experienced handlers, often people who have devoted a lifetime to breeding, picking the right ones, and then showing those dogs through to their championships. Moreover, the most perfect Poodle ever born

ISABELLE FRANCAIS

Miniature Poodle Best of Breed winner of the Westminster Kennel Club Dog Show 1994. This is Ch. Surrey Sweet Capsicum owned by Robert A. Koeppel and bred by Mrs. James E. Clark, Mrs. J. Furbush, and Mr. K. Hosaka.

NECK
strong and long enough to allow dignified carriage.

SKULL
moderately rounded; definite stop.

EYES
very dark, oval in shape.

EARS
close to head, leather long, fringe not of excessive length.

FOREQUARTERS
strong and smoothly muscled.

FORELEG PUFFS

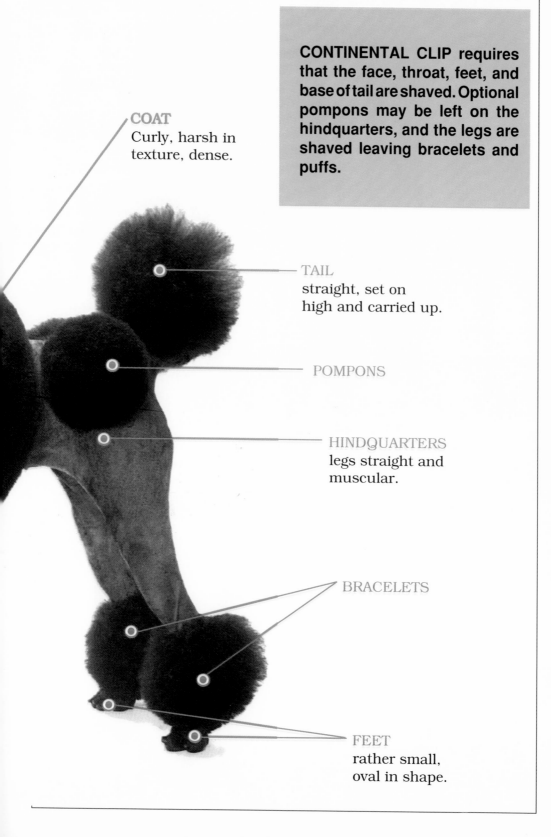

CONTINENTAL CLIP requires that the face, throat, feet, and base of tail are shaved. Optional pompons may be left on the hindquarters, and the legs are shaved leaving bracelets and puffs.

COAT
Curly, harsh in texture, dense.

TAIL
straight, set on high and carried up.

POMPONS

HINDQUARTERS
legs straight and muscular.

BRACELETS

FEET
rather small, oval in shape.

has faults, and in your hands the faults will be far more evident than with the experienced handler who knows how to minimize his Poodle's faults. These are but a few points on the sad side of the picture.

The experienced handler, as I say, was not born knowing the ropes. He learned—*and so can you!*

ISABELLE FRANCAIS

Learn to set your Poodle up to show off his best assets. Experienced handlers will also know how to off-balance a dog's lesser qualities by accentuating the positive!

You can if you will put in the same time, study and keen observation that he did. But it will take time!

KEY TO SUCCESS
First, search for a truly fine show prospect. Take the puppy home, raise him by the book, and as carefully as you know how, give him every

ISABELLE FRANCAIS

Pay attention to your Poodle while in the ring. Dog shows must be fun for the dogs or else why bother? Also don't forget to watch the judge and be ready to do whatever he or she asks of you and your dog.

chance to mature into the Poodle you hoped for. My advice is to keep your dog out of big shows, even Puppy Classes, until he is mature. Maturity in the male is roughly two years; with the female, 14 months or so. When your Poodle is approaching maturity, start out at match shows, and, with this experience for both of you, then go gunning for the big wins at the big shows.

Next step, read the standard by which the Poodle is judged. Study it until you know it by heart. Having done this, and while your puppy is at home (where he should be) growing into a normal,

ISABELLE FRANCAIS

Fortunately for Poodle folk, Poodles are naturally showy animals. Most Poodles will stand by themselves without having to be "set up" by their handlers. Judges are always delighted by a natural showman.

healthy Poodle, go to every dog show you can possibly reach. Sit at the ringside and watch Poodle judging. Keep your ears and eyes open. Do your own judging, holding each of those dogs against the standard, which you now know by heart.

In your evaluations, don't start looking for faults. Look for the virtues—the best qualities. How does a given Poodle shape up against the standard? Having looked for and noted the virtues, then note the faults and see what prevents a given Poodle from standing correctly or moving well. Weigh these faults against the virtues, since, ideally, every feature of the dog should contribute to the harmonious whole dog.

"RINGSIDE JUDGING"

It's a good practice to make notes on each Poodle, always holding the dog against the standard. In "ringside judging," forget your personal preference for this or that feature. What does the standard say about it? Watch

Outdoor shows have become more and more popular, especially in the cool months. This handsome class of Standard Poodles are in the process of being evaluated at a dog show.

carefully as the judge places the dogs in a given class. It is difficult from the ringside always to see why number one was placed over the second dog. Try to follow the judge's reasoning. Later try to talk with the judge after he is finished. Ask him questions as to why he placed certain Poodles and not others. Listen while the judge explains his placings, and, I'll say right here, any judge worthy of his license should be able to give reasons.

When you're not at the ringside, talk with the fanciers and breeders who have Poodles. Don't be afraid to ask opinions or say that you don't know. You have a lot of listening to do, and it will help you a great deal and speed up your personal progress if you are a good listener.

THE NATIONAL CLUB

You will find it worthwhile to join the national Poodle club and to subscribe to its magazine. From the national club, you will learn the location of an approved regional club near you. Now, when your young Poodle is eight to ten months old, find out the dates of match shows in your section of the country. These differ from regular shows only in that no championship points are given. These shows are especially designed to launch young dogs (and new handlers) on a show career.

Agility trials test not only the intelligence and training of a dog but also the natural agility and the owner's rapport and communication with his dog. These Poodles are taking the bar jump at an exciting agility competition.

ROBERT PEARCY

There is much talk these days about the intelligence of dogs. Poodles have always ranked among the very smartest of dogs and can compete on all levels of competition. These Poodles are competing in the Open class at an obedience trial, the high jump and the broad jump.

ENTER MATCH SHOWS

With the ring deportment you have watched at big shows firmly in mind and practice, enter your Poodle in as many match shows as you can. When in the ring, you have two important jobs. The first is to see to it that your Poodle is always being seen to its best advantage. The second job is to keep your eye on the judge to see what he may want you to do next. Watch only the judge and your Poodle. Be quick and be alert; do exactly as the judge directs. Don't speak to him except to answer his questions. If he does something you don't like, don't say so. And don't irritate the judge (and everybody else) by constantly talking and fussing with your dog.

In moving about the ring, remember to keep clear of the other dogs beside you or in front of you.

It is my advice to you *not* to show your Poodle in a regular point show until he is at least close to maturity and after both you and your dog have had time to perfect ring manners and poise in the match shows.

Winning at a dog show is but one of the advantages to investing in training your dog. In addition to the ribbons and recognition, training your dog can bring you much personal satisfaction, and your Poodle will be happier and wiser too.

T.F.H. Publications, Inc., offers many quality books that all Poodle fanciers can enjoy. *The Book of the Poodle* is a comprehensive colorful guide to the breed, and *The Poodle,* highly regarded by Poodle exhibitors, was written by Poodle judge Anna Katherine Nicholas. Also available is *All (132) Breed Dog Grooming, The Atlas of Dog Breeds of the World, Canine Lexicon, The Mini-Atlas of Dog Breeds* and *Everybody Can Train Their Own Dog.* Each of these award-winning books are available in pet shops and include hundreds of wonderful color illustrations.